Military In Transition's Guide to The Survivor Benefit Plan

By Forrest Baumhover

Table of Contents

Preface

So, why did I write "Military In Transition's Guide to the Survivor Benefit Plan?" After all, you can Google SBP and see that the DFAS website comprises pretty much all of the page one rankings. And it should.

Reason One. To better understand what you need to know about the Survivor Benefit Plan. Everything you can read on the DFAS website is technical content. This book attempts to balance that with a more personal touch based upon real life scenarios and case studies. The DFAS website doesn't attempt to understand the intricacies of military life. This ebook does attempt to do that by bringing content that's easy to identify with, and I hope it succeeds.

Reason Two. This book attempts to organize some of the pertinent SBP information into a single document that is easy to read. If you look at the DFAS website, it has almost all the information you need to do the hard calculations. However, the DFAS website is also so disorganized that it frustrated me into writing this book. You'll note that the last part to this ebook is a simple compilation of all of the pages from the DFAS website in one easy to navigate appendix. There is a DFAS guide, which is pretty hard to find on the website, since it seems to be hidden away with no apparent links to it. You can reach it right here; however, reading it is less fun than reading 50 pages of the tax code. No wonder people get frustrated with SBP—they can't even stay awake long enough to get through the guide! Hopefully, this book gets the point across more clearly.

Reason Three. This book looks at SBP from both sides. There are some people who will say, "You should ALWAYS go with SBP," while there are some people who say, "You should NEVER go with SBP." **The truth is, it depends on your situation,** and it's hard to tell unless you walk through some of it wearing other people's shoes (or hypothetical shoes, since some of these case studies are fiction). This book won't make the decision for you, but I hope it gives you some perspective so you feel better equipped to make the decision for yourself.

Reason Four. You deserve this! When I was going through all of this content, I kept thinking, "I deserve better than this!" You do too. We've all been there...whether you're in the Army, Navy, Air Force, Marines, Coast Guard, Reserves, or National Guard. Over the past decade and a half, our armed forces have gone through an unprecedented operational tempo of deployments, separation, and loss. SBP is one of the entitlements our servicemembers have been granted by an Act of Congress, and we deserve better than to suffer through a bunch of stuffy text and a cursory speech during the firehose we call Transition Assistance Program. No offense to our TAP counselors, but when you go through several dozen speeches and lectures in a week, they all seem watered down, even if they're chock full of action-packed content. Which SBP is worth a separate effort to highlight the key considerations about the decision-making process.

I hope you enjoy this; however I do ask one favor. This costs $4.99, which is less than the cost of a 6" Subway sub. I hope it is way more satisfying. Seriously, though, if you're worried that buying this book will cause you to go a day without that Subway sub, let me know and I'll see what I can do. And if you send me an email within 30 days of your purchase telling me that this was just the worst $5.00 you've ever spent, I'll happily refund your money. My primary job is being a fee-only financial planner. However, if spending a couple of bucks on a book that nudges you in the right direction saves you hundreds of dollars in financial planning fees, then it's worth it to me.

My number one goal is to serve this community, so please either tell all your friends how great this is, or tell me how I need to fix it. Again, I hope you enjoy this book!

Forrest

Chapter 1 – What is the Survivor Benefit Plan (SBP)?

Let's start talking about SBP. Nothing more than the basics here: why is SBP important, the terms, etc. Think of this as a primer to start the rest of the conversation in this book.

Why is SBP so important and why was it established?

When a military retiree passes away their pension automatically stops. Without a plan to replace this lost income, the family's quality of life, or even their livelihood, could definitely be at risk.

SBP was established by Congress in 1972 specifically to help military retirees and their families protect themselves from the risk of financial loss if the retiree were to die before his family did. As we'll get into in the next chapter, it's clear that Congress' intent in establishing SBP, and its reserve component counterpart, RC-SBP, is to provide *annuity* income to protect against the financial loss of the retiree, presumed to be the primary breadwinner in most families.

You said SBP is an annuity. What is an annuity?

Great question! The best way to describe an annuity is to compare it to a life insurance policy. Although insurance gets VERY complex, below is an attempt to break down what an annuity is by using the simplest terms.

Life insurance provides a specific sum of money (eg. maximum SGLI of $400K) to your beneficiary if you die. That beneficiary can then use that insurance payout to help make up for the income you would have otherwise earned had you stayed alive. Buying life insurance is like you're betting the insurance company that you'll die before your family has enough money to live on. If you die and your family gets a payout, you 'win.' But not really.

In contrast, an annuity is guaranteed income for life. You buy an annuity by giving the insurance company a bunch of money (either at once, or in regular payments over time). In exchange, the insurance company promises that it will start paying out on a guaranteed date. If you live long enough to make your money back (or more accurately, more money than you'd have if you took your payments and invested them separately), you win. Keep living, and the insurance company keeps paying. That's great, and it sounds so much better than an insurance policy.

I get the annuity part, but why is SBP so hard to understand?

First, SBP is an annuity that acts like a life insurance policy. Unlike most annuities, SBP only kicks in after the retiree passes. If both spouses die at the same time, or the retiree outlives the spouse, you don't get a dime from SBP. Companies with defined benefit plans (think your grandfather's gold watch & pension) are required by law to provide a Qualified Joint and Survivor Annuity (QJSA), which acts a lot like SBP, in that it pays a percentage of the retiree's pension to the retiree's spouse. However, those plans are about as rare as gold watches at retirement anymore. I just doesn't happen in today's day and age. **Also, there's not really anything comparable to SBP in the insurance industry, so it's hard to find civilian references or financial planners that can help you determine whether it's right for you.** All the necessary information is available from government sources. However, when you try to research it online, it can be difficult to piece together.

For example, the DFAS website has a ton of information, including a Survivor's Benefits Guide[i]. However, the guide is so hard to find that I had written four articles on everything I thought I found on the DFAS website before I *found* it. The only reason I stumbled upon DFAS' SBP guide is because I Googled "SBP guide" to see if anyone had written a book like this one before. It's not anything I would have found intuitively on the DFAS website. It doesn't even show up when you search for the title: 'GUIDE TO SURVIVOR BENEFITS.' You have to search for 'SBP Guide.' So, that's frustrating.

As for the rest of the information, it's not really organized in the best manner. So, at the end of this ebook is a compilation of DFAS's SBP webpages, just organized in a format that's a little more navigable. I didn't try to recreate anything or interpret anything. Hopefully, it's a little easier to digest. Please email me if you see anything out of place.

Also, as I previously mentioned, there isn't a whole lot of time spent on helping people understand SBP during TAP class. TAP class is a firehose of all things you need to understand about your transition, and SBP is just one in a list of myriad topics that need to be discussed. That doesn't mean that SBP isn't important, it just means that there isn't enough time in the TAP curriculum to give SBP the focus that it deserves.

Finally, although DFAS administers the SBP program for DoD, each service is tasked to inform and educate their eligible servicemembers. As a result, it can be confusing to figure out where to go for guidance. The service-specific instructions, as well as the OSD instruction, can be accessed in Appendix 3.

What are the terms of SBP?

Under SBP, the servicemember pays a certain percentage of retired pay (currently capped at 6.5%, depending on family status, but perhaps less in certain cases) in exchange for the right for beneficiaries to receive 55 percent of the servicemember's retirement pay upon death. For simplicity's sake, we'll use 6.5% as the SBP premium rate here and in the examples in this book.

If the servicemember has $1,000 per month in retired pay, the SBP premium would be $65 per month. Upon death, the beneficiary would receive $550 per month. However, after 360 months and reaching the age of 70, the servicemember is considered 'paid up' and there is no additional cost to you. SBP coverage is in place for life, and there are no more premiums due. It's important to note that a retiree must pay into SBP for 360 months AND be 70+, so people who retire in their late 30s (i.e. enlisted in their teens) could pay into SBP a little longer.

That's it. That's the basic premise. It's pretty simple to understand, until you get down into the details and 'what-ifs' that life throws your way. Then, it can get very confusing and frustrating. In this book, we'll attempt to discuss some of these 'what-ifs' and look at some real-life scenarios & case studies that might resemble your situation.

In Chapter 2, we'll take a look at the history of SBP, and some of the societal changes that have impacted SBP's role in today's military family. This will help us better evaluate what types of financial issues SBP can address, and what it cannot. This way, you can start to get a better understanding of what role SBP should play in your post-military life.

Chapter 2 – The Impact of History on SBP's Relevance in Today's Military

Let's pull back a bit from SBP itself, and take a look at how society has changed over the past 40+ years since SBP's inception. We'll identify the risks that were most prevalent in the 1970s, when SBP was created, and see how societal trends have altered some of these risks. By taking the time to look at these risks, we'll be better able to figure out where SBP plays a role.

Workforce demographics

According to the Department of Labor's Facts Over Time-Women in the Labor Force[ii], less than 44% of women were present in the labor force in 1972. As women began to enter the workforce in greater numbers, this statistic trended upwards until it reached 59.9% in 2000. It has since settled down to the mid to high-fifties (57.7% as of 2012), but it's clear there are more women in the workforce than there were a generation ago. At the same time, DOL's statistics show a slight decrease in men's workforce participation, from 78.9% in 1972 to 70.2% in 2012.

Women as the primary breadwinner

I could have lumped this in under workforce demographics, but I wanted to point out a very significant statistic. In 2013, the Pew Research Center released a study[iii] indicating a then-record 40% of women as primary breadwinners for their family. Of these women, 37% were women who outearned their husbands, while 63% were single mothers. The share of women primary breadwinners was just 11% in 1960.

Longevity increases

People used to work for a very long time, then retire, collect a pension for a couple of years, then die. However, people keep living longer and longer. As a result, most companies, and eventually the U.S. Government, realized that longevity increases will only continue. In 1999, Congress passed legislation to allow for a 'paid up' provision, so that people could stop paying into SBP after 30 years. The intent was to keep enrollment rates up by allowing people to avoid paying into SBP for 40 or 50 years (which is completely plausible in today's society) with little or no benefit. According to the World Bank[iv], the U.S. life expectancy for males went from 67.4 years in 1972 to 76.5 years in 2013. For women, the life expectancy went from 75.1 years to 81.3 years over the same time period. For an average married couple, the difference in life expectancy went from 7.7 years to 4.8 years.

This is a double-edged sword. This indicates that more servicemembers are paying the full 30 years' SBP premiums. At the same time, female spouses of retired male servicemembers may not be outliving their spouses as long as they did a generation ago, which might reduce the total lifetime benefit.

Health care costs

While we're living longer, it comes at a price. According to data compiled from the World Bank[v] and the Centers for Medicare & Medicaid Services[vi], the US' health care costs (as a percentage of US GDP) rose from around 7% in 1970 to 13.2% in 1995 to 17.1% in 2013. A lot of this increase has to do with better technology, better medicine, more specialized health care, and the fact that older people have more complex health issues. However, as these trends continue, we can expect health care costs to continue to increase. This does not include the costs of long term care or any non-medical costs associated with getting older.

Aging parents

As life spans increase, and health care costs rise, many people end up having to take care of their parents, even as they're raising their children. In addition to the increased stress, this can limit a person's lifetime income potential if they have to take substantial amounts of time off from work, take on a lesser paying job, or completely stop working in order to take care of their parent. It also adds a direct financial strain if they have to pay out of pocket for long term care. While these don't have a direct relationship with SBP, the financial strain and opportunity costs are both insurable needs that need to be addressed.

Same sex marriages

Now that same-sex marriages are nationally legalized, it's important to understand how this adds complexity to your individual situation if you are in a same-sex marriage. Many of the traditional issues and concerns (like a female spouse worrying about outliving her servicemember husband) might not apply in same sex marriages. In one of the mini-case studies, we'll look at an example of a same sex couple and evaluate their situation in more detail.

Second careers

Although there are not statistics readily available, it's safe to say there are more military retirees taking on full-length second careers (20 years or more) after their military retirement than in the 1970s. Long gone are the days where people like my grandfather retired after 30 years as an O-6 and didn't take a second job. Now, it's not just everyone whose pensions aren't enough to completely retire. O-6s and general/flag officers almost always take on a second job, even if it's as a part-time consultant. Creating job security for such retired officers is so prevalent that it's a phenomenon known as "No O-6 (or GO/FO) left behind." Google it.

Retirements later in life

Not only are more career servicemembers taking on second careers, but those careers are lasting longer and longer. Many military retirees are working until their mid-late 60s into their 70s and beyond. It's not clear whether this is a microcosm of society's gradual shift towards later retirements, or whether there's another cause. One observation is that there are many more white-collar jobs than there were a generation ago, and much more employer flexibility to accommodate the schedules and inclinations of people with the experience and education that many retired servicemembers offer.

Income parity between married couples

The assumption used to be that the income was directly tied to the military career. As more military members marry high income-earning 'dependents,' this assumption is no longer the case. You could find that the military person is not the primary breadwinner if married to a doctor, lawyer, or other professional.

College tuition

There are more high school graduates going to college than there used to be. According to Familyfacts.org[vii], the percentage of adults age 25 and older with a college degree has skyrocketed from less than 10% in 1965 to over 30% as of 2011, the latest date this data was available. That makes sense, since college is pretty much seen as a necessity in today's job environment.

College is also more expensive. According to College Board[viii], a non-profit organization that "connects students to college success and opportunity," the average annual tuition for a four-year public school (in today's dollars) more than tripled, from $2,387 in 1975 to $9,410 in 2015. The tuition for a private school also tripled, from $10,088 in 1975 to $32,405. When you add room and board, you can count on doubling, if not tripling those expenses.

As a result, people are taking out student loans in record amounts. According to Debt.org[ix], student loan debt rose from $260 billion in 2004 to over $1.2 trillion in 2014, for an average of $33,000 per person. And it's not all college students, either. The number of people over 60 with student loan debt has more than tripled to 2.1 million, responsible for $43 billion of that debt. Up to 5% of those over 60 are having student loan payments taken out of their social security checks. As a result, higher college costs directly lead to less retirement assets being available to support you down the road.

Marital status changes

According to a Washington Post article on marriage and divorce rates since the Civil war[x], marriage rates were at an all-time low in 2011, the latest date that information was available in this report. Surprisingly, although divorce rates spiked in the 1980s, there was a subsequent decline in divorce rates in the 1990s and early 2000s. As a result, divorce rates are about the same as they were in 1970. However, the overall trend is that today, a smaller percentage of America's population is married than in 1970.

It's important to recognize these trends, as they come with changes that stray from the original purpose of SBP: **to provide for the sudden loss of income by a spouse (predominantly female) when the retiree (primarily male) passes away.** Later on, we'll see some case studies that turn the concept of SBP completely on its head. By understanding how these trends may apply to your personal situation, you can start to conceptualize some of the ways in which SBP may (or may not) be right for you.

In Chapter 3, we'll take a look at SBP from an insurance point of view, and evaluate what types of financial issues SBP can address, and what it cannot. This way, you can start to get a better understanding of what role SBP should play in your post-military life.

Chapter 3 – Insurable Needs

Before we start discussing SBP again, let's identify some of the post-military risks that today's servicemembers & their families face. Once we do that, we'll be better able to figure out which risks SBP addresses, and which ones it does not. To better imagine these risks, we'll list them in order of what you're most likely to experience as you go through life.

Immediately after military retirement

Most people in this category are probably between 40 & 50 years of age, but this isn't exact. Let's define this as the group of people who are retired, aren't yet financially independent, and still have a lot of debt or expenses related to raising a family.

For most people, you're in your prime earning years. You've got a military pension, but you've also got big bills. Mortgage payments, children, college planning, taking care of aging parents…braces, for goodness sakes! You're working to live, and lucky if you're able to set aside some savings. You do the right things…pay yourself first, invest a part of every pay raise, work down consumer debt. All of that is to keep your family's engine going.

What happens if the primary breadwinner dies? You lose income, but you also lose the potential to build retirement savings. In essence, you lose the primary earning years—those years in your 40s and 50s where you've maximized your earnings potential, and have yet to be sidelined by age-related issues that force you to slow down.

Cash flow: Income stops, but the bills don't

Emergency fund: What happens if you get a double whammy: primary breadwinner dies, coupled with a car accident? Or worse, a triple whammy, where your oldest child's tuition is now due? You've got a sudden need for a large amount of cash, RIGHT NOW.

Close to financial independence, but not quite

This group has gotten through raising their kids, and they probably no longer have to care for their parents. However, they've still got a mortgage, and are still building their retirement nest egg. If they had to, they could 'retire,' but they'd always be one minor issue away from a financial crisis. They've got another 5-10 years to really get to the point where they can afford to retire and have a life.

> *Cash flow*: Their cash flow needs aren't as bad, but they still need to have some cash flow.

> *Emergency fund:* It's not as likely that a 'triple whammy' will happen, as most of the expenses left the house when the kids did. As long as they're on track to have successful lives of their own, you can even tolerate one or two 'boomerang' kids.

Retired

Whether it's financial independence, or you've gotten close enough to collecting Social Security that you're able to make it work, you're retired (or able to retire with a part time 'hobby' job). Now your concerns are oriented towards making sure that your income can cover your needs and support your post-retirement goals & dreams.

> *Cash flow:* You're at the point where you've got no major bills (or close to that point), and your retirement assets, plus your pension & Social Security, provide all the income you need.

> *Emergency fund:* This is no longer an issue. Financial independence includes having enough money to address emergencies as they arise, no matter what they are.

Advanced age

These are the sunset years. Now you're not as mobile, and long term care is on the horizon, if it's not already here. Medical care costs are rising. Your primary concern is making sure you don't outlast your money, and that you've got something left over in your estate for your loved ones.

> *Cash flow:* Your care expenses might be starting to eat into your retirement savings. Hopefully, you've got enough left.

Emergency fund. There isn't a whole lot that isn't anticipated here. Your biggest concern is paying for emergent medical issues.

Estate planning

This isn't really a point in life that should be 'at the end,' but a lot of people really don't think about their estate until they're knocking on heaven's door. Ideally, you've addressed your estate throughout your life, but if not, you're probably thinking about it right before you're going to pass. Hopefully, you have enough time to make sure your affairs are in order.

No insurable needs at all

Perhaps you don't have any family members. Your parents have passed away, and you've been totally dedicated to your career, so you never got married or had children. Or, perhaps you're no longer married, and your children are grown up and no longer dependent on you for support. In this case, you might not have an insurable need.

Below are some insurable needs that don't seem to fit into any age-related category:

Special needs: I won't attempt to categorize this any further, but most people recognize whether this pertains to their situation. If it does, you may find that a special needs trust is appropriate. However, you should consult a lawyer and/or a financial planner who specialize in working with special needs families to determine whether one is right for you.

Disability: Disability could happen to anyone at any time. We're all familiar with the VA disability claim, even if no one (or it seems like no one) understands the 'black box' where our claims go in and come out of. Sometimes, you can find yourself in a similar situation with your employer. Injury on the job may prevent you from being able to work at your full capacity, so you file a disability claim.

One difference: in the military, anything that isn't expressly ruled out is considered 'in the line of duty,' since we're in the military 24 hours per day. However, a civilian employer won't see disability in the same way. So if you get into a car accident on your way home from work, and now you can't do your job anymore (whether it's driving a forklift or flying a plane), what happens?

Long-term care: You might be looking into this for your parents. You might be looking into this for yourself (even if it's a ways off). However, long-term care is expensive, whether you're talking about long term care insurance, or self-insuring and paying the bills yourself. Or, if you can't afford it, it takes a physical & emotional toll on the family member who's responsible for the care.

Funeral & probate costs: Estate planning is one thing. However, having a funeral is expensive in itself. Also, if your will is probated (which can be avoided with proper estate planning), your executor/executrix will have to hire a lawyer to do the legal work. If it's contested, this could go sideways really quickly and cost a lot of money.

Aging parent care: As previously mentioned, having to care for aging parents, either financially, or through time that could have been spent earning additional money is an insurable need that you should take into account.

Now that we've identified some insurable needs, let's discuss what options are available to address them.

Chapter 4 – How We Can Address Insurable Needs

In Chapter 3, we discussed some of the insurable needs that come up at each stage of post-military life. Now we're going to take a look at some of the ways that we can mitigate those insurable needs. Let's frame this discussion in terms of investing in SBP, or taking that same amount of money and seeing what else we can do with it. Let's remember the basic premise of SBP:

Premium: $65.00 per month per $1,000 of covered pension

Payout: $550 per month per $1,000 of covered pension

Now, let's evaluate SBP and other alternatives to identify pros and cons of each.

SBP

This is what this book is about, right? We understand what it costs, because I just mentioned it above. So, let's get down to discussing the pros and cons.

Pros:

- Provides a guaranteed, monthly payout for the lifetime of the beneficiary
- Indexed for inflation. This means that the payout will rise with the cost of living adjustment (COLA) as long as it continues to be paid
- Predictable, and therefore, can be used when determining cash flow in financial planning.
- Once in 'paid-up' status, no longer require payments. Paid-up status occurs after 30 years (360 months) of premium payments AND reaching age 70. There may be circumstances where a retiree pays for 30 years and has to keep making payments because they have not yet reached age 70.

- Once selected, SBP premiums are automatically paid from pension (or VA compensation by filing Form 2891 through DFAS)

Cons:

- No access to principal
- Payments stop upon death of the beneficiary. In most cases, this is the spouse, so when the spouse dies, there's no residual benefit for adult children (except in special needs cases, in which the child can become the beneficiary in certain qualifying circumstances)
- Payments are taxable
- If beneficiary predeceases retiree and there is no other qualified beneficiary, coverage stops unless retiree remarries.

Term Life Insurance

A lot of financial planners will discuss SBP in terms of how much life insurance you could buy with the SBP premiums. We use term life insurance because it's cheaper and less complicated than other insurance products out there. Most financial planners (other than insurance salesmen), generally agree that term policies are the most appropriate type of life insurance for the vast majority of people.

Pros:

- Term life insurance covers the 'prime earning years,' as part of a financial plan. At the end of the policy term, it is expected that a family will be financially independent. They will have accumulated enough money so that neither term insurance nor SBP are needed.
- Lump sum payment can be used to address emergent issues
- Payout can also be invested to generate cash flow. The amount of cash flow generated depends on a variety of factors, including investment rate & payout amount. Cash flow amount may be more or less than the SBP payout based upon these factors
- Tax-free proceeds

- Can be assigned to additional beneficiaries if the primary beneficiary predeceases, or dies shortly after the insured
- Terms can be assigned for various periods, from 10-30 years

Cons:

- After the term expires, the policy is no longer in force. A new policy must be written, most likely at a higher rate. If no new policy is written, there is no longer an expected benefit.
- If premiums stop being paid, the policy could lapse, leaving an uninsured risk.

Savings

You could pocket the difference. In this case, that difference is $65 per month for every $1000 of protected pension. Assuming an 8% interest rate, you could have the following:

After 10 years:	$11,301.68
After 20 years:	$35,698.99
After 30 years:	$88,370.97

Those amounts are for each $1,000 in protected pension, so you'd have to recalculate based upon how much your SBP premium actually would be. For example, instead of protecting a $4,000 pension, your SBP premium ($65 X 4 = $260) would amount to $353,483.88 at the end of 30 years. This could be in tax-advantaged accounts (such as an IRA), or after-tax accounts. Let's look at the pros & cons.

Pros:

- You have money in pocket.
- Savings accessible for emergencies (although possibly subject to taxation on gains and/or other limitations, such as early withdrawal penalties on tax-advantaged accounts)
- Can be assigned to secondary beneficiaries if both retiree & spouse die.

- This is a really good deal if both the retiree and spouse die at the same time or within a short period of time of each other. If this were to happen, the savings component would outweigh the SBP payout.

Cons:

- No one knows when they're going to die. So, how likely is it that both spouses will be able to plan on dying at the same time?
- In early years (and even over the long run), the available savings will most likely not be able to outweigh the payout from either SBP or an insurance policy.
- It's easier to 'dip' into this money and use it for other things. If this happens, then the money won't be able to serve its intended purpose.

Annuity

I'm not going to break out the pros and cons here, because I don't see much plus side in this kind of situation. There are some people who believe that an annuity might be appropriate. Without going into too much detail, I'll state that **SBP IS an annuity, even if it acts like a life insurance policy**. I'll also say that many financial planners advise people to stay away from most annuities. In this case, we're talking about setting aside a little bit of money (in SBP's case, approximately 12% of the expected monthly payout) each month, in exchange for a certain payout upon the retiree's death. Annuities are subject to high sales charges, commissions, and surrender charges.

When you look at the numbers, it's highly unlikely you'll find an annuity product in the marketplace that will compare with SBP.

Bottom line: Unless both spouses outlive the 30-year term, choose not to renew their life insurance policy (because at that point it would be much more expensive) AND die at relatively the same time, the benefits of 'just saving the premiums' don't justify the risks. There are too many scenarios in which your family might not be able to support their needs in case something happens.

There are a lot of insurable risks that we didn't cover here. For example, long term care, and long term disability are two risks that neither

SBP nor term insurance (not considering riders that can accompany a life insurance policy) can adequately address. However, both of those risks represent the same real threats:

- Losing lifetime earnings potential
- Not being able to pay bills and support current needs
- Not being able to save for retirement

With that said, we'll continue this conversation as if we're comparing the benefits of SBP vs term insurance from here on out. In the next two chapters, we'll discuss some situations in which SBP might be appropriate for you, and when it might not be your best choice.

Chapter 5 – Situations Where SBP Might Be Appropriate

Now that we've discussed some of the risks and drawn a comparison between SBP & term life insurance, let's discuss some real-life situations for which SBP might be appropriate. As a caveat, this is not an all-inclusive list. It's simply a starting point for identifying factors which might warrant considering SBP.

Budget is a priority. You can budget for it. You won't like it when you find out how much of your retirement pay gets pulled into taxes, TRICARE, SBP, etc. However, once you budget for it, you can move on. In today's day & age, most people are retiring with enough time to make a full second career and not miss too many meals because they're paying into SBP.

Planning. You can plan for SBP. If you die, you know what your spouse is entitled to. Knowing this helps you plan your other income requirements accordingly. Factoring SBP into your estate planning helps you mitigate the financial needs that you have to address.

Uncertainty. You don't know the future. You don't know when you're going to die, and you don't know what the investment landscape will look like when you do. If you're under 50, odds are that the retirement landscape is going to look MUCH different than it does today. SBP is a hedge against that uncertainty.

You're more concerned about the sunset years than the mid-life years. If you have confidence that you can make it through your 40s and 50s, but you're a little concerned about what life will look like if you're a sudden widow(er) in your 60s or 70s, then SBP might be right for you. However, be careful to ensure that you've got a plan to account for that income gap you might have in your prime earning years.

If you're male. If you're a male (in 2013, approximately 85% of the active duty workforce was male), odds are your spouse will outlive you. With everyone living much longer today, odds are that your surviving spouse will get much more benefit out of SBP than you pay into it while you're alive.

If you're uninsurable or if you have a medical rating that raises your insurance premiums. As we'll discuss in one of the case studies, we'll go into detail on how a term insurance can protect you. However, that's not a whole lot of consolation if you're not able to obtain insurance in the first place, or if your medical rating makes term insurance too expensive.

If you're overweight, drink a lot or a smoker. This isn't to pick on people, but insurance companies will take lifestyle choices into consideration when setting premiums, so it's worth mentioning here. And if you've got 20 years' worth of smoking history in your medical record, they'll pick up on that during the underwriting process, even if you put 'No' on your application. However, SBP doesn't have any underwriting, and you pay the same rates as you would if you were in relatively good shape, and never drank or smoked a day in your life.

If you're older. As you get older, term insurance becomes more expensive. Take a look at VGLI as a proxy (not an exact measuring tool), and you can get the point....price increases are gradual in your 20s and 30s, but in your 60s and 70s, they become very cost-prohibitive. If you're an older retiree (like many reservists, people with broken service, or senior enlisted/officers), you might find that term insurance is a much more expensive option for you.

If your family has special needs children. According to the DFAS Guide[xi], SBP/RCSBP is payable to a incapacitated son or daughter over age 18 if the condition happened while the child was a minor (or under age 22 and enrolled in a full-time course of study). This is a great help to families of special needs children, as SBP can be used as an estate planning tool after the parents have passed away.

If age difference is a significant factor. We've already discussed how SBP benefits female beneficiaries of male retirees. However, if age is a significant factor, then SBP starts to make sense in same-sex relationships, or relationships where the female servicemember is significantly older than the male. Since the SBP payoff is somewhere under 4 years, this might be worth looking into in relationships where the age difference is 5 years or more, regardless of sex.

If you're afraid of blowing through all of your money. One of our case studies is based upon the 'Erin Factor.' The Erin Factor, which we'll go into more depth on later, is the situation where the beneficiary feels so uncomfortable being around money that they would rather have an annuity without access to the principal, specifically so they don't ever have to worry about running out of money. Even if term insurance is a more financially appropriate solution, the Erin Factor indicates that the right answer is the one that allows the beneficiary to sleep at night, even if it means less money in the long run.

Now that we've covered situations in which SBP might be appropriate, let's take a look at the flip side in the next chapter.

Chapter 6 – Situations Where SBP Might Not Be Appropriate

Now that we've discussed some of the risks, and drawn a comparison between SBP & term life insurance, let's discuss some real-life situations or reasons in which SBP might not be appropriate. As I mentioned in the previous chapter, these points of discussion are just that: reasons you might want to consider not enrolling in SBP.

You're looking to see whether your SBP premiums could be put to use in a better manner. This point isn't to 'declare victory.' However, if you're skeptical about SBP and grudgingly sign up, then you're probably not going to be any happier at year 15 wondering why you dumped your money into it. If this is the case, then you should look into a term insurance policy, understand the risks, and proceed accordingly, or you can put your money into savings and call it a day. You should probably only do this after lots of analysis and consideration. *Bottom line: No one's forcing you into SBP.*

Planning. You can plan for SBP. You can also plan for a term insurance policy. Think of the term expiration as if it were a deadline for financial independence. Plan as if you won't need the SBP payout by the end of the term and you're protected just in case.

You're more concerned about getting to your sunset years than you are about living in retirement. If you have confidence that you'll have enough money in retirement, but your focus is getting the kids through college, paying off the mortgage, and just collecting a little retirement fund before you're too old to work, then a term insurance policy is a good hedge 'just in case.' However, be careful that you've got a plan beginning in Year 1 after the term expires.

If you're female. If you're a woman (using last chapter's stats, in 2013, approximately 15% of the active duty workforce was female), odds are you'll outlive your spouse. With everyone living much longer today, odds are not in your favor if you're looking to break-even or get more money out of SBP than you put in.

If you're insurable and healthy. If you're able to obtain insurance, and you don't have any medical issues that will raise your premium, you may find that you can purchase a lot of insurance for the same amount as your SBP premium. This could be a huge consideration as we'll see in the next chapter.

If you're younger. Younger people can lock in cheap insurance for 30 years, then just work really hard so that when their term expires, they no longer need it. If you're retiring in your early 40s (or in many enlisted cases, late 30s), you might find yourself in this position.

If age difference is not a significant factor. If you're in a same-sex relationship, or a female servicemember relationship, you may already be leaning away from SBP. However, if you're pretty close in age AND you're in one of these relationships, this might be the deciding factor for you. As we discussed in a previous chapter, the life expectancy between men and women has started to shrink, which might impact your expected SBP benefit.

Now that we've covered some of the hypotheticals, let's look at a few case studies. First, we're going to talk a little (well, a LOT) about a situation in which term insurance seems to make sense over SBP (don't worry, there's a flip side to this argument).

Chapter 7 – Case Study #1: My Personal Situation

As I discussed in my article this chapter is based upon, I originally wrote this as an analysis for my personal situation, when our family was pondering SBP vs. term insurance. I probably could have saved myself a LOT of hassle, had I known that the DoD Office of the Actuary annually publishes a calculator that does the analysis for you. You can find the most current version here.

While we've already gone over most of the caveats below in previous chapters, I will outline them again here. I want to make a very clear impression that this is not an attempt to make people feel uncomfortable with a decision they have already made, but to help illuminate the way ahead for those who are still weighing their options.

Peace of mind should be your number one priority. If SBP is your answer & nothing will change your mind, do not read further.

Investment risk. If even the thought of some investment risk (even US Government-backed securities or bank CDs) scares you, **stop.** While this discussion goes into scenarios with very low, achievable investment returns, which can be reasonably achieved with very safe investments, such as a treasury bond ladder or CDs, nothing is ever guaranteed.

Inflation. This analysis assumes fairly low COLA (inflation) rates. This could change, and should be considered accordingly. However, the assumptions are generally in line with inflation rates used by financial planners.

Risk. This analysis ONLY addresses the financial risk associated with the loss of pension income before we've accumulated enough retirement assets to support living expenses. For this example, I'm more concerned about my wife raising our 3 children and paying the mortgage if I die in my 40s than I am about cash flow needs in our 70s. By the time we reach retirement age, our plan is to not have to rely upon my pension (or SBP payout) for her to afford her living expenses. If this doesn't sound like your goal, you should reconsider whether this is an option for you.

Types of risk protection. To the above point, term insurance and SBP provide unique protection against different types of risk.

- Term insurance protects against the sudden cessation of pension income while you're still building your retirement assets. It does this much more effectively than SBP.
- SBP is a longevity hedge. It provides guaranteed protection regardless of how long the surviving spouse outlive the retiree. In this case, SBP protects against a risk that term insurance does not.
- However, there is a mutual benefit that SBP and term insurance provide—**the ability to generate a stream of income.** That is the focus of this comparison.

Spouse protection. Neither SBP nor the term insurance policy protect against the financial concerns that arise if the retiree outlives the spouse. For example, such a financial concern would be having to budget & pay for child care, or to replace that person's income. For female servicemembers or servicemembers married to someone with chronic health concerns, this is a huge issue. It might be worth considering purchasing a term insurance on the spouse to protect against this risk.

This situation assumes that at the end of a 30-year term policy, you will have enough accumulated retirement assets to offset your SBP benefit. **If you're not comfortable with the fact that in Year 31, your pension could go to zero, stop.**

This analysis assumes your insurable need is for a 30 year term policy. You may find lower rates (or a higher insurance policy for approximately the same premium) if you're willing to accept a 20 year term, which some people may be willing to do if they are older and closer to financial independence.

Insurance Cost. This analysis doesn't try to compare whether SBP is cheaper than insurance. I'm using information from my previous article, where I outlined how much insurance I would be able to purchase with the amount of money I'd otherwise use for SBP. In this case, for the same premium ($260 per month) I'm able to purchase either:

- SBP coverage on a $4,000 pension
- 30 year term policy valued at $1.5 million

You may find that you can buy more or less insurance, based upon your particular situation. **Whether you die at Year 1 or a Year 29, you will have paid approximately the same amount (after tax) for either outcome.**

Taxation. This analysis assumes that SBP proceeds are 100% taxable, while the insurance payout is not. However, earnings on the principal are taxable. We will assume a 25% tax rate.

Special needs. This analysis does not assume any special needs, or any situations other than what I explained above. You should establish a relationship with a financial planner who specializes in special needs before trying to determine whether SBP is appropriate for your situation.

Analysis: If your situation is significantly different from the one outlined above, you may have to do your own analysis to figure out what is right for you. **In fact, you should do your own analysis anyway. It is YOUR life and you need to OWN your decisions.**

Caveats out of the way, let's get to work comparing the two scenarios.

Calculating distribution: Instead of assuming a flat distribution rate as a percentage of the insurance proceeds, we're comparing the guaranteed $2,200 monthly pension (adjusted annually for cost of living adjustment increases), to how long a $1.5 million policy would last if set aside and used to match the after-tax SBP payout. For example, at a 4% annual COLA, the $26,400 in Year One will become $27,456 in Year Two. After tax, this becomes $19,800 and $20,592, respectively. The distribution from the lump sum investment will match this, first with earnings, then with principal. The calculations reflect the tax impact from earnings, but zero taxation on principal.

Returns: We will make changes to the SBP COLA and hypothetical investment returns for the payout. These hypothetical investment returns are very low. In fact, the highest rate, 4%, is a generally accepted distribution rate in the financial planning industry that still allows for the long-term preservation of capital. However, anything above the US-Government 30 Year Treasury rate (currently at 2.75%) involves some sort of investment risk, however slight. These returns are labeled 'Income' on the graphs below.

COLA: If the SBP COLA is higher than the investment returns on the insurance payout, then SBP will become the more financially sound option more quickly. However, if the COLA lags behind the investment returns, then the insurance payout will outperform SBP. The below illustrations attempt to compare and contrast a couple of scenarios in which COLA is higher than the payout investment returns, and vice versa.

Break-Even: Using a side-by-side comparison of the payout numbers allows for us to analyze the 'break-even' point, or the point at which the COLA-adjusted SBP pension become a better financial option than a lump sum payout. The break-even point is defined as the year in which the invested lump sum, which replicates the SBP payout, is depleted. After the break-even point, SBP is the better option. Any shorter, and the term insurance is more attractive. To clarify:

AFTER Break-even: SBP wins

BEFORE Break-even: Term Insurance wins

For the illustrations used here, I've used a 40 year time horizon. At the bottom of each illustration is a bullet point summary of how much money you would have at the end of this period, as well as the SBP break-even point.

Illustration 1

Illustration 1 represents the break-even point with an annual COLA of 4%. 4% is a very high inflation number, especially in light of recently low COLAs. However, most financial planners do factor a 3-4 percent inflation assumption for long term projections. Using 4% represents the highest inflation rate most professionals would reasonably use. **Note:** In the early 1980s, inflation was in the double digits, so 4% is not a 'worst case scenario.' However, it's reasonable to project that 4%

annual adjustments will be the highest we expect to see over a 30-40 year time horizon.

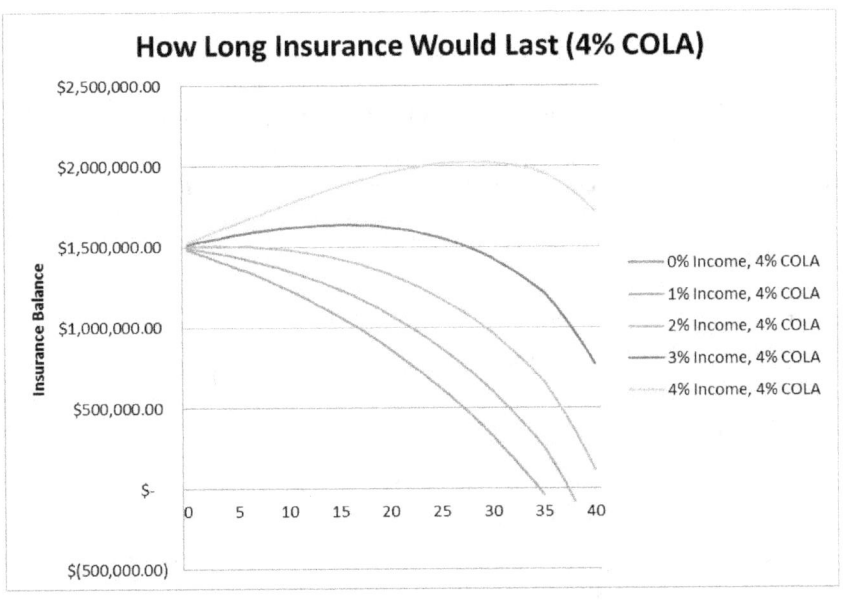

How Long Insurance Would Last (4% COLA)

As you can see, even with a 4% COLA, there is no situation in which a $1.5 million portfolio would last less than 30 years. The SBP break-even point is at least 35 years for any of these scenarios. Even if you took the money and put it under a mattress, you would be able to match the COLA-adjusted SBP payout for 35 years. And at a 4% income, you end up with more money than you started with at the end of 40 years! Although it's not in the chart, 30-year Treasury rates were around 2.75% as of March 11, 2016, so you could safely assume a return somewhere between the 2% and 3% lines. Assuming you did not build a bond ladder (which staggers bonds with maturity dates, so that you're continuously reinvesting as each bond matures, and taking advantage of rising interest rates) and only received the current Treasury rate, you would still have almost $600,000 at the end of 40 years.

Numbers below: Amount after 40 years
        Breakeven Point

0% Income $ 0-Run out of money at 35 year mark   35
1% Income $ 0-Run out of money at 38 year mark   38

2% Income	$ 114,437.54	40
2.75% Income	$ 584,267.18	44
3% Income	$ 772,879.56	45
4% Income	$ 1,725,825.83	53

Illustration 2

Illustration 2 is calculated the same way as Illustration 1, but with a COLA of 2.3%. Why? It was hard to find any single document with the historical COLAs for military pensions. In fact, I couldn't find any DFAS press releases older than 2011 showing the next year's increases. Here's what I found:

2012: 3.6%
2013: Couldn't find it online
2014: 1.5%
2015: 1.7%
2016: 0

I understand that DoD COLA tracks very closely to Social Security increases. However, instead of approximating a COLA based upon 30+ years of Social Security tables, (available at: https://www.ssa.gov/news/cola/automatic-cola.htm, I decided to turn to an 'informal' source. The first lead I found was from Mike (no last name listed) at Military Pay. Mike's website has a retirement calculator, and according to his FAQ, he's incorporated previous COLA rates, and uses a projected rate for future earnings. Based upon my napkin math, this projected rate appears to be 2.3%. So that's the projected COLA rate for this illustration.

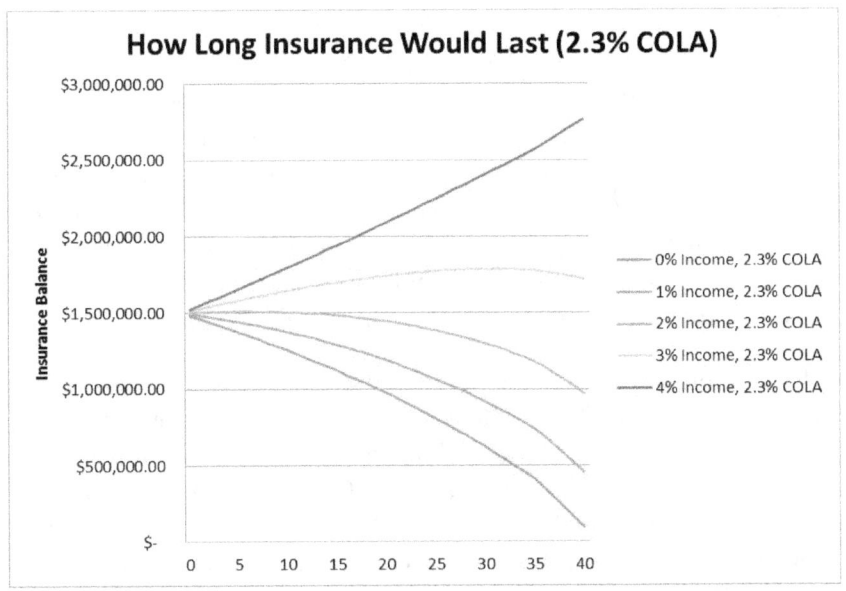

How Long Insurance Would Last (2.3% COLA)

Legend:
- 0% Income, 2.3% COLA
- 1% Income, 2.3% COLA
- 2% Income, 2.3% COLA
- 3% Income, 2.3% COLA
- 4% Income, 2.3% COLA

In this illustration, you can see that there is no scenario where this payout does not last 40 years. Again, even if all you do is dole out money from under your mattress to match what you'd have received from SBP, you'd still have money left over at the end of the scenario. At the 30-year Treasury rate of 2.75%, you'd have your starting amount, and at 3%, you'd have more money than you started with.

Numbers below:	Amount after 40 years	Breakeven Point
0% Income	$ 95,576.94	41
1% Income	$ 453,168.59	46
2% Income	$ 972,722.41	54
2.75% Income	$ 1,504,953.05	63
3% Income	$ 1,715,799.71	68
4% Income	$ 2,725,825.83	108

Liquidity

Another important aspect to the insurance versus SBP discussion is the matter of liquidity for beneficiaries. Spouses--if you're hit with a sudden loss, AND you need money to pay bills, AND you haven't been in the workplace for a long time, you may need money if your SBP payout cannot cover your living costs. You will need time to deal with EVERYTHING that happens…dealing with all of the things that happen when you lose a loved one, as well as addressing your entitlements, all while trying to keep your household in order. Your SBP payout probably won't be enough to deal with all of this. You may find yourself raiding retirement assets to pay ordinary bills. Having a low-cost, term policy in place can help you through that first year or two of adjustments that you'll be making as you prepare yourself for the rest of your life. One reason that I drew out such unrealistic projections (such as the 108 year timeframe in Illustration 2) is to show that even if my wife took a big chunk of money to just get through that first year, she'd still be financially prepared.

For example, let's imagine my wife used $500,000 to do whatever she needed to do, and had $1,000,000 set aside to provide her annual income. In the worst case scenario (4% annual COLA, that she matches with under the mattress money) that $1,000,000 would still be able to match the SBP payout through year 27. Instead of 108 years, $1,000,000 would get her through Year 57 under the 4% income, 2.3% COLA scenario. *In addition to providing a means for a steady income, an insurance policy gives you flexibility to address immediate needs...SBP cannot offer this.*

Although these projections seem outlandish, they may not be as longevity increases keep pushing the boundaries of our life expectancies. There are plausible situations where my wife could outlive me by 50-60 years, and need income into her 100s. However, that scenario is not as much of a concern to me as the liquidity and immediate cash flow concerns.

Conclusion: In this scenario, a term insurance policy seems to be a more financially sound option than SBP. However, if I predecease my wife by 30 years or more, she might be better off with SBP. With that said, 30 years gives my wife plenty of time to take control of her life after my demise, and to find the help she needs to move forward with her financial life. Also, I don't plan to have my wife outlive me by 30 years.

In the next chapter, we'll look at a scenario in which SBP was by far the best option, and where the beneficiary (my grandmother), was able to live a long, fruitful life because of the plan that she and my grandfather put together.

Chapter 8 – Case Study #2: My Grandmother's SBP Experience

In Chapter 7, I outlined a case study for which a term insurance policy would be preferable to participating in SBP. This chapter serves to provide a completely opposite viewpoint. In this chapter, we'll use my grandmother's SBP experience as an example. While I do not plan to follow this example in my personal situation, I do think it's important to demonstrate how SBP could work when the military spouse outlives the retiree by a number of years.

My Grandmother's Background

My grandparents were both World War II vets. Being of the Greatest Generation, they were fairly frugal people. When my grandfather retired from the Army as an Army O-6 after 30 years, they settled down in the Florida house that he (and eventually I) grew up in. Since this house was inherited from his father, they had very minimal expenses. Also, since he entered active service well before September 8, 1980, he was entitled to retire at a percentage of his Final Pay, vice High Three. Finally, they were of the age where second careers were almost non-existent…they retired from everything & anything that involved a job. My grandmother was still very active in our small community, and my grandfather kept busy just by maintaining his house and their property. My grandfather died in 1983, while my grandmother lived until 2011, so she enjoyed 27+ years of SBP payments.

This case study will attempt to project what a person in a similar position would have earned if this scenario happened today. However, so this can be relevant to everyone, I'll also break down an illustration of this payout per $1,000 of protected pension. That way, you can adjust based upon what you expect your pension to be. If you'd like a copy of the Excel file so you can make your own calculations, please feel free to ask me. To make this case study relevant to today's audience, we'll make a few adjustments:

Instead of going through previous years' records, we'll calculate what my grandmother would have received in today's dollars, if my grandfather passed in 2016. We'll then project the next 27 years and show the total earnings.

As previously indicated, there will also be an illustration of payout "per $1,000 of protected pension." This should allow you to prorate the amount based upon your particular situation.

We'll use a standard COLA rate of 1.5%, even though historical rates were either much higher (like in the 1980s) or somewhat lower (like 2016's 0% increase).

We will not calculate the cost of SBP, just the amount of benefit.

These illustrations will project both pre-tax and post-tax earnings, based upon a 25% tax rate. You may have to adjust your projections based upon your marginal tax bracket.

Caveat: This is a projection based upon an assumed 1.5% annual COLA rate. Most likely, actual results over the next 40 years will not reflect this projection.

Let's Begin!

As you may recall, SBP pays out $550 in monthly income for every $1,000 in protected pension. If your pension is $2,000 per month, the spousal payout would be $1,100. The below illustrations shows the COLA-projected payout, both annually & lifetime accumulation, *per $1,000 of protected pension* over a 40 year time horizon.

My Story

If you recall, my projected pension is about $4,000 per month. Decent pension, but definitely not the kind of money we could retire with, like my grandparents. A complete loss of this income, though, would mean not being able to pay the mortgage (or any expenses). Here's what I'm looking at, below:

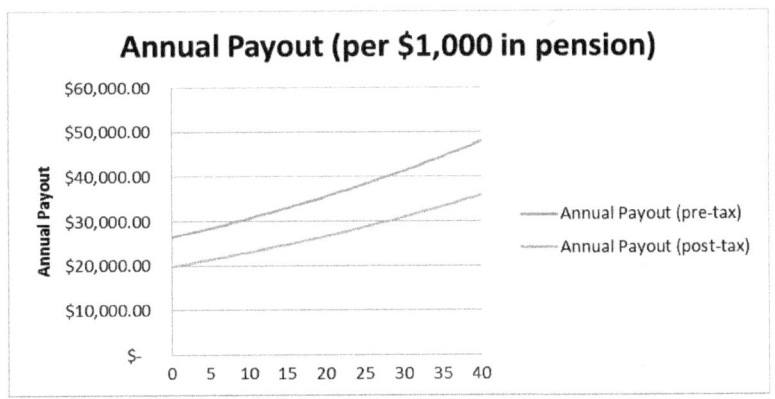

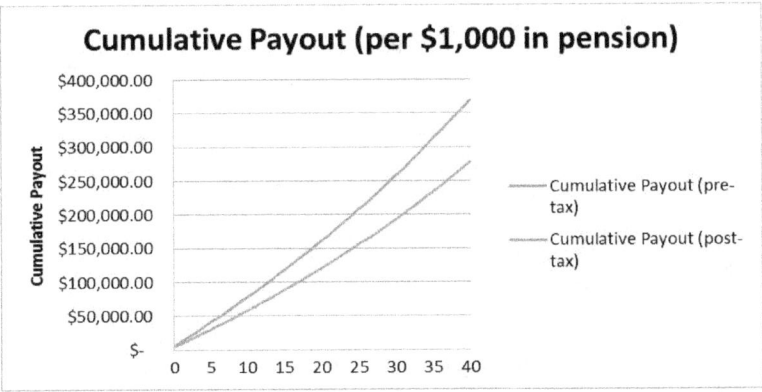

I'm probably going to go with a 30-year term life policy because if I die, my wife would receive around $20,000-$25,000 in SBP benefits (in today's dollars). That is not nearly enough to support our living expenses. However, the amount of money we would receive from the term policy would equal about 40 years' worth of SBP benefits. Let's see how my grandmother fared.

My Grandmother's Story

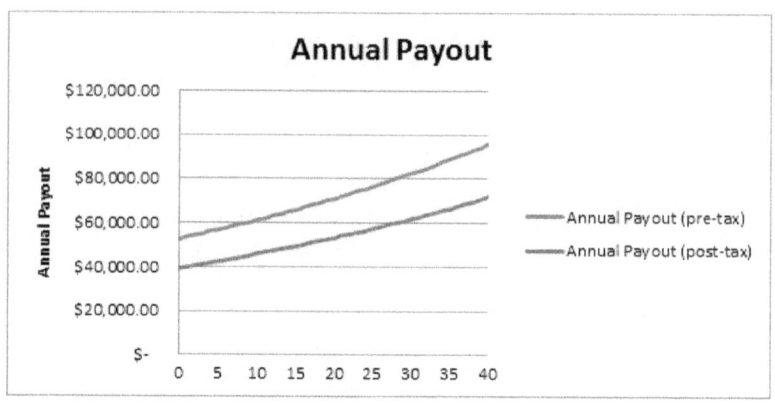

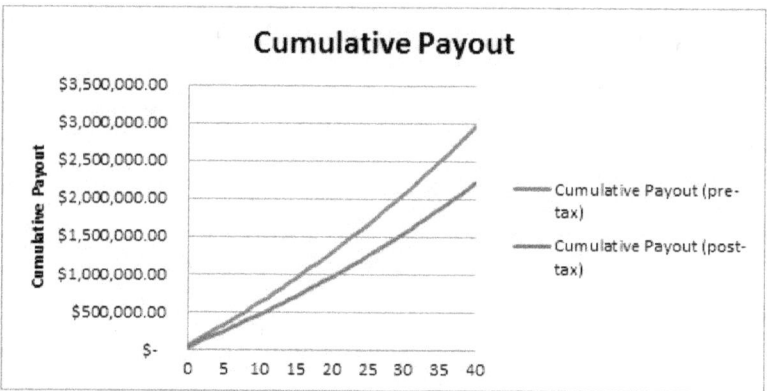

While this is more than what my grandmother ACTUALLY received, this is a present-day example of what a person in a similar position could expect to receive. For her, receiving $40,000 (post-tax) was enough to support her needs. Of course, she had no mortgage, her children were grown, she bought a car every 10 years with cash (whether she needed to or not), and she lived in rural Florida, where cost of living was cheap. However, more important than the amount of money she received was the fact that she *never lost a minute's sleep* worrying about finances after my grandfather died.

As you can see, these two cases are extremely opposing scenarios, and ones in which the answer is pretty evident. In the upcoming 'mini-cases,' we'll explore a couple of hypothetical situations and walk through the analysis to get to a conclusion.

Chapter 9 – Mini Case Studies

Below, there are five hypothetical situations that might be similar to those of people you know. You might not see any of them as the 'typical' military family, but each scenario probably contains one or two things that you've seen at some point in your life. This chapter doesn't intend to impose an opinion one way or another, but merely to inform you about some of the factors you should take into consideration in each case.

Each case will outline the background of a hypothetical service member and his or her family. At the end of the case is the same question: Which would be the preferred option, SBP or a term insurance policy, and why? This isn't a 'universal' answer, but my recommendation, as well as some of the rationale behind it. Feel free to make up your own mind in each case, but I hope this expresses some of the critical thinking that goes into each recommendation.

Note: As mentioned previously, you can use the insurance calculator on the OSD Actuary website to compare term insurance to SBP, and I would recommend doing so in each personal situation.

Let's start with our first case, which is an older military couple looking to retire after 30 years.

Mini Case #1

Master Sergeant John Smith and his wife, Tiffany, are looking to retire after 30 years of service. They are about the same age. Their children are now adults living independently, and they've built up a decent sized nest egg for retirement. MSgt Smith plans to take on a second job as something to keep him busy and to make sure they can retire the way they want to, but won't commit to a career choice.

Tiffany has been working as a licensed practical nurse (LPN), which has allowed her to work wherever they've been stationed. They have a house, which they first bought earlier in their career. At this point, they've built enough equity in their home so that they can sell it (which they intend to do) and buy a smaller home in cash, although they're looking at a mortgage so they can keep their money working for them. Tiffany has indicated that she's comfortable with where they are financially, and is more interested in a guaranteed income than 'getting the most from her money' if her husband were to die before her.

MSgt Smith does have some medical issues. He has type II diabetes and a family history of strokes. Additionally, he had a hip replacement after a terrible parachute accident earlier in his career. As a result, he isn't able to run as much as he used to, and is slightly overweight. He's been trying to quit smoking, but has promised that he'll definitely quit when he retires.

He has gotten some life insurance quotes, which indicate that he would be covered, but with a medical rating. This means that his life insurance would come at a higher cost than someone else of identical age without the medical concerns.

Which would be the preferred option for the Smiths: SBP or a term insurance policy for MSgt Smith, and why?

In the Smiths' case, I would probably recommend SBP for the following reasons:

- They don't really *need* the money from an insurance payout, since they no longer have children at home, and their only major expense (a retirement house) can be paid for by the cash proceeds of their old home. They both plan to work, and would have income and an emergency fund to address most unanticipated needs.
- Due to MSgt Smith's medical rating, it's unlikely they'll get a decent policy for the same amount of money that they would pay into SBP premiums. If they do get a policy, it likely will not generate the same amount of income that SBP would.
- It's likely that Tiffany will outlive her husband, especially if he doesn't get his weight down and take control of his health. If he lives into his 70s and she still outlives him, then SBP gives her assured income into her retirement years.
- The most important reason: Tiffany says she'd rather have a guaranteed amount of money that she can plan on than trying to see if she can get more money from an insurance policy.

Mini Case #2

Navy Captain Susan Jones is planning to retire after 25 years. Her husband, Brian, is a few years younger than Susan, and their children are teenagers. After a dozen tours of moving around, they're looking forward to finally buying a house of their own in Washington D.C. where she'll work as a defense contractor and he can finally put that doctorate degree to work as a professor. They're counting on her pension as well as their dual incomes to really ramp up their retirement savings for the next 20 years, and then they'll retire back to Susan's home town in Texas.

They've paid down their debt (mostly), but are looking to fund most of their children's college education, if they can. Neither spouse has any significant medical issues.

Which would be the preferred option for the Jones family: SBP or a term insurance policy for Susan, and why?

I would probably lean towards term insurance in this case for several reasons:

- It's likely that Susan Jones is going to outlive her husband, who would not receive any benefit from the SBP premiums.
- Susan's term policy could be reassigned to their children if Brian were to predecease her.
- As a woman in good health, Susan would probably be able to obtain enough insurance to meet the following needs:
  o Emergent needs. Possible need to fund college & pay mortgage costs if Susan were to predecease her husband.
  o Generate savings for Brian's retirement years.
  o Cash flow. Susan's policy could generate cash flow that would likely be in excess of the SBP payout.

Mini Case #3

Marine Gunnery Sergeant Matt Evans, and his husband, Steve, are planning to settle down after 20 years in the Corps. Matt's proudly served his country, as Steve did before he got out 10 years ago. However, Matt is eager to support Steve's career as commercial real estate agent.

Since they moved to Norfolk 5 years ago, Steve has really taken the bull by the horns and is now earning an income well in excess of six figures. They've got plenty of money saved up, thanks to frugal living and dual incomes over their 10 year relationship. If they stopped working now, they would have enough emergency money saved up to pay their current living expenses for at least five years without dipping into their retirement accounts. After retirement, Matt doesn't know what he'll do yet, but he'll 'find something.'

Matt & Steve have no kids, nor do they have plans for any. They're both the same age (40 & 41, respectively). They've got a nice condo in downtown Norfolk, which they bought at a bargain 4 years ago when the real estate market tanked. They're both in excellent health, as they're both rabid Crossfitters and compete in several events per year.

Which would be the preferred option for Matt & Steve: SBP or a term insurance policy for Matt, and why?

Quite frankly, you could argue that neither is the best option for a couple of reasons:

- Matt & Steve are REALLY close to financial independence, if not already there yet. We don't have numbers, but knowing that they could pay 5 years of living expenses WITHOUT going into their retirement accounts is a big indicator. Most financial advisors suggest having 3-6 months living expenses, so Matt & Steve are well ahead of expectations.
- Being a same-sex couple means a lower likelihood of one outliving the other. Also, they're pretty close in age, so there's not a longevity risk here.
- It appears that even though Matt is the service member, he's actually more dependent on Steve than vice versa. If a term insurance policy makes sense, it would be to protect against the sudden loss of Steve's six-figure income, not Matt's E-7 pension. Insurance rates would likely be comparable, so you might as well put it to the best plausible use, or at least hedge your bets by putting a policy in place for each person.

This was a purposefully tricky situation, since there are a couple of things in here that you probably wouldn't have seen 20-30 (or even 5-10) years ago. There are:

- Same sex families

- Many 'dependent' spouses who out-earn their military spouses
- Military couples not having children. This allows them to save more money and be in a position to declare financial independence earlier in life.

Mini Case #4

General David Abrams and his wife, Jessica, are getting ready to retire after 30 years of service to the Washington DC area, where he's wrapping up a tour at the Pentagon. They just got married 5 years ago when she left the Army. They met in Fort Hood, Texas while he was a colonel and she was a first lieutenant. Shortly after she got out of the Army, they got married and had the first of three children. He's 53, and she just turned 30.

Gen. Abrams is looking at several consulting jobs in the DC area. He plans to work for another 5-10 years, then retire for good so he can spend some time with their children before they go off to college. They've got a decent amount saved up, and they've already bought a house. Jessica has completely set aside her professional goals to raise their children.

Which would be the preferred option for the Abrams family-SBP or a term insurance policy for General Abrams, and why?

I think this is a pretty clear case for SBP (although a retired general might be able to afford a term insurance policy as well). Here are the reasons:

- He's older than someone retiring in their forties, so like MSgt Smith, the insurance company might charge a higher premium for his coverage. He's not so old that insurance doesn't make sense, but SBP probably makes more sense.
- Unless something unusual happens, Jessica is almost surely going to outlive her husband, and it's not even close. Plugging this situation into the OSD Actuary website, there's a 94% chance that Jessica survives her husband's death.
- Not only will Jessica likely outlive General Abrams, there's a great chance that she'll collect SBP for a LONG time after he dies. A scenario like this (extreme, but there are many

older male/younger female relationships, particularly amongst men in second marriages) could have the female beneficiary collecting SBP for 40-50 years.

Mini Case #5

This is our last case, known as the 'Erin Factor.' This case study is based upon a real-life scenario that was brought to my attention by Jennifer Lear, a lawyer and an accredited financial counselor. We'll go into this case study, which I created, then more in depth with the real-life story for which "The Erin Factor" is named, as well as some suggestions on how you could address the concerns that come up.

Army Colonel Steve Jones and his wife, Erin (for simplicity's sake) are about to retire after 26 years of service. They're pretty successful financially, and have saved a decent amount of money. Medically, COL Jones is in good shape, and relatively young, at 47 years of age. Erin is 50. There aren't any issues that would preclude him from becoming insurable at a reasonable cost. As a retired colonel, their pension would be about $7,000 per month.

The Joneses have no children, nor any parents to care for. Their townhome is almost paid off (ten years left), and they have no car loans or student loans. In addition to COL Jones' salary, Erin is a successful doctor, and is able to just buy what she needs, when she needs it. Since they live a relatively modest lifestyle, they don't stick to a budget or really watch their expenses.

Over the course of their career, they've had SGLI, but Erin has always wondered what she would do if $400,000 just 'fell into her lap' unexpectedly. Her biggest fear is that she'd blow through the money within a couple of years and not have anything for the rest of her life. This fear is compounded by the fact that she largely distrusts financial planners, or anyone selling financial advice. She had a couple of friends who were burned by some 'financial advisers' that sold them a bunch of expensive annuities, and she doesn't want to end up in the same situation.

Which would be the preferred option for the Joneses: SBP or a term insurance policy for COL Jones, and why?

This looks like it could go either way, and I would rely upon the OSD Actuary website to help figure out which one makes more sense financially. Quite frankly, Col Jones' pension is enough that he could protect some of it with SBP, buy a smaller term insurance policy, and still come out all right. That way, he protects himself during the term period, but ensures a pension that Erin can count on. Let's look a little further here:

- **You should pick the best option for you, financially.** That's why I'm a huge fan of going to the OSD Actuary's website. Here, you can get a pretty good determination of what's in your best interest, based upon life expectancies and all of the other calculations that go into making this decision. In this case study, I put in a bunch of information that you could use to go into the OSD Actuary's SBP/Insurance calculator, but you still have to play around with some numbers. Let's plug in some more assumptions, and see where this goes.

  - **Surviving spouse income bracket.** Since the Joneses are pretty well off, and they will accumulate more wealth, we can assume that investment income will keep them pretty high. Oh, and Erin is a doctor. Let's assume they're not necessarily in the highest bracket (39.6% for married filing jointly making over $466,950 in 2016). However, let's assume they're in the 33% bracket.

  - **Inflation & interest.** For inflation and interest rates, OSD's Actuary Website sets a default rate of 2.75% and 5.25%, respectively, for the long term. Use whatever you want, but I don't see much reason to change them here. 5.25% is a very reasonable assumption for long-term investment returns in a balanced, well-diversified portfolio (most planners use 6-8% for long-term growth projections).

  - **Insurance amount.** This is a tough one without going through the underwriting process. However, take a look at the SBP premium on COL Jones' pension, which is $460 per month. Even the max VGLI premium (which is considered expensive) for a 45-49 year old is $88 per month for $400,000 in coverage (in 2016), so you can assume that COL Jones can lock in a pretty decent rate for a 20-year policy. According to USAA's website, a 47-year old retired man can get about $3,000,000 coverage for $386.64, which is less than his SBP premium. Let's assume he qualifies for half that amount, or $1,500,000, or even though there aren't any red flags that would cause him to qualify for less coverage.

Using this information, there is no time during the 20-year term in which SBP outperforms the insurance policy. However, being able to hedge your bets could put your mind at ease. With that said, there are still a couple of questions.

- **What happens if he should outlive the term policy?** This is a very valid question. In this case, the Jones' would have addressed their insurable need, which is protecting Erin during her most valuable years. Having that insurable need fully addressed would then allow them to focus on their retirement goals. There is no reason why they would reach this point without being close (if not already at) financial independence. Having part of the pension protected by SBP helps mitigate this. This brings us to Question 3.

- **I don't trust myself, and I don't trust 'financial advisers' with money.** This is the focal point of this entire case study, and the most important consideration for this decision. The 'Erin Factor,' as I briefly mentioned, is the phenomenon in which a surviving spouse fears that she (could be a he, but most men don't seem to have this concern) will suddenly not be able to manage the money that she has come into, and will be left broke and destitute within a few short years.

This is a valid concern, especially if you've had one person managing the finances. There are any number of questions that come to your mind, and any one of these would erode your confidence. To that, I'd offer a couple of points to let you know that you CAN do this:

  - **There's no secret formula to managing money.** My family is in the same boat. My wife, Tania, trusts me to do all the investments, while she does all the shopping. This isn't a jab on Tania, but we long ago agreed that we don't need two people buying stuff in the family. She manages the budget because she runs the household and knows what we need to keep it going. That's natural, right? All she asks is for me to keep an eye on the investments and insurance needs. So, she basically has an approximate budget that we stick to each month. If I died, there would be some adjustment to that number, but it's still a number that she'd eventually live with. I don't really have any secrets, and have everything written down so she'd know what we need to do if I kick it. If you still don't think you can manage it yourself, then let's go to the next point.

- **If you're afraid you're going to blow an insurance payout, what makes you think you're going to handle a pension any better?** I don't mean to ask this facetiously, but the main counter-point to this question is that you can't outspend a pension. True. But, if you're worried about spending $500,000 or $1,000,000 in a few short years, how will you be able to handle $2,000 or $3,000 per month? Everyone knows they could responsibly handle the latter, but the insurance payout is so large by comparison that it becomes intimidating. It's a mental challenge, but at the end of the day, you could lock up most of a $1,000,000 insurance payout in CDs and pay yourself $3,000 a month. Even at 0% interest, you wouldn't run out of money for 27 years. So, perhaps you need someone to help you.

- **You can set up your insurance proceeds so that you can't spend down your money.** If this is truly a concern for you, you and your spouse can consult a lawyer to help you create a trust, specifically to safeguard your principal and provide income for your beneficiaries. Such a trust, funded by your insurance policy is known as an irrevocable life insurance trust, or ILIT. While a financial planner can help you determine whether a trust is necessary for you, only a lawyer can establish and advise on the specific legal aspects of a trust.

- **You can hire a financial planner to hold you accountable.** If you don't want to go through the hassle of establishing a trust, but you still want some sort of accountability measure, you can hire a financial planner. Holding clients accountable is a little known job (collateral duty, really) of a financial planner. If you're paying someone, you're probably going to be less likely to go to your quarterly meetings feeling like you aren't prepared on your end. It's like cleaning up your hotel room before housekeeping arrives. You're all right with a little mess, but you're going to be pretty embarrassed if you trashed your room the night before, and you're still in the room when the maid arrives to clean it for you. Find someone that you know, like, and trust, and that has your best interests in mind, and hire that person to help you gain control of your finances. That leads to our last question.

- **I don't know if I can find someone that I know, like and trust.** This is a legitimate question, and kind of based upon the opinion of a lot of do-it-yourselfers. There are plenty of military people who choose to manage their own finances (and do so quite successfully), because the military lifestyle forced them to. It's hard for financial advisers to maintain relationships with their clients if the clients keep moving, so a lot of advisers don't even try. After a while, do-it-yourselfers often stop seeing the value of a financial professional because they didn't need one. Also, the fact that the financial services industry is one of the least-trusted and most confusing doesn't help the matter. Every time I read a story about one of 'those commands,' I just shake my head knowing that this is a bad representation of the industry.

However, there is a difference between a do-it-yourselfer and people who identify with the 'Erin Factor.' The difference is that the latter probably does need professional assistance, whether as a one-time effort to give them a baseline and a checklist, or as an ongoing relationship to manage obstacles that life throws their way. Either way, finding a trusted professional is straightforward. Also, many financial professionals, especially younger ones, are starting to leverage technology, such as Google Hangouts and Skype, to develop and nurture long-distance relationships with their clients.

- First, start with your friends, family, or relatives. Odds are, you might know someone who really likes their financial adviser. Ask that person what makes them happy about their relationship. If their answer really inspires you, you should strongly consider that person. Clients who are referred to a financial adviser by an existing client tend to be happy clients. If no one in your circle of friends has an adviser, perhaps your mentor does.

- Second, start with another professional you trust. Do you have a lawyer, real estate agent, or accountant? Maybe. If you do, you could ask their office for a referral. All of these professionals work with financial advisers, and their referrals are a direct reflection of their professional reputation. If your accountant wants to maintain your trust, they're probably not going to refer you to someone who will burn you.

- Third, look online. Ha ha. No, really. The National Association of Personal Financial Advisers (NAPFA), is the world's largest association of fee-only advisers. Fee-only advisers charge their clients based upon fees. Fee-only planners receive no commissions from sales of insurance or investment products. NAPFA has a step-by-step guide on how to find a financial adviser. This guide has a checklist of informed questions that you can ask to ensure that the person you hire does have your best interests in mind.

- Fourth, ask me. I'm a financial planner, and I'd be more than happy to see if I can help you. If I can't, I'll do my best to put you in touch with several financial planners who might be a better fit for your situation. Feel free to email me directly at: forrest@westchasefinancialplanning.com.

A little about the 'Erin Factor,' which is a legitimate concern. Jennifer Lear, whom I previously mentioned, coined this phrase for a lawyer-friend of hers who is in a similar (not identical) situation as the one I outlined above. Although she and her husband are successful, 'Erin' is mortified that she will blow through any insurance proceeds, and believes that SBP will help her because it protects her from herself.

So, if you've reached this point and you're still not convinced that you should give up your SBP, then don't. You're not the only one, and I'm by no means trying to advise people to take or forego SBP. My goal is to make sure that you make an informed decision. It all goes back to the number one priority: peace of mind. Your peace of mind should drive everything behind the financial decisions that you make.

Summary: I hope these case studies showed some of the analysis that you should do (or have a financial planner do with you) to come to the right answer. You'll note a couple of hot-button topics that I did not even attempt to address: divorced families & special needs cases. Each of these represents situations in which there are any number of legal complexities, which can vary based upon which state you live in. If either of these situations applies to you, and you have even the slightest uncertainty, you should consult the legal documents (such as your divorce decree or trust documents). If you have further questions, you should sit down with either a lawyer or financial planner specializing in that field to help you understand the legal and/or financial aspects of those situations.

Thank You Page

This is usually known as the Acknowledgements page, but that never sat well with me. If you're walking down the hallway and see a complete stranger, you acknowledge their presence. That's not what I wish to do here. I want to thank all the people who made this possible.

First and foremost, my wife Tania. Tania is my life partner, and I'd never have made it through my military career (at least without a couple of NJP charges) without her. Also, my three children, Nicholas, Emma, and Jackson—raising you guys is by far the greatest accomplishment I could possibly wish for!

My mother & my grandmother, who raised me (a pretty difficult task). My mother worked very hard as a cleaning lady to make sure I had clothes, food, and housing. My grandmother took me in at a very young age and provided a lot of the inspiration for the direction I eventually took in life (although I joined the Navy instead of the Army). Thank you both!

My friends and fellow financial bloggers in the online community. Doug Nordman, Ryan Guina, Kate Horrell, Rob Aeschbach, Jennifer Lear, and so many more people embraced me as a new blogger and writer, took me under their wings, and really helped encourage me through every step. Writing a book is easy. Writing a good book and getting it out to the right audience is a whole different story, and I'm so thankful to my fellow writers who pushed me to keep going. Thanks Rob, for helping me create the Military In Transition Facebook Group—I'd have never done it without you! Doug, thanks for that one post where you told me I should turn my articles into an eBook in the first place! Thanks Ryan, for that initial conversation, where you introduced me to a whole new world of achievers. And thanks Kate, for poking me in the eye when my opinion differed from yours. Instead of annoying me, it made me refocus and write better. Jennifer, thank you for sharing your experience as a financial counselor, and thank you for helping me create a case study based upon the 'Erin Factor!'

Of course, all of the people in uniform, whether it be yesterday, today, or tomorrow. On a personal note, everyone has mentors, shipmates, foxhole buddies, or subordinates who all help to form them as a person. After spending my entire adult life in uniform (I turned 18 in boot camp), I owe a lot of who I am to the military. However, long after I'm retired, there will still be that 20-year old standing watch, or the 30-something dependent spouse trying to hold their family together during an extended deployment. At some point, *everyone wearing a uniform hangs it up eventually.* This book is for each of you.

Appendix One: SBP Website (The Whole Dang Thing in One File)

Advantages & Disadvantages

Advantage: You will leave a guaranteed income to your beneficiary
Eligible beneficiaries under the plan will receive 55 percent of the retiree's elected amount of coverage.

Advantage: SBP benefits are inflation indexed, and coverage and cost are not affected by illness or age
Unlike many private life insurance policies, SBP coverage will not be cancelled or revoked due to any illness you may have or your age. Whether you retire at age 45 or 80, you or your spouse's age or health will never be considered a liability and never impact the cost of the program. In addition, the receipt of survivor benefits will not be affected by Social Security benefits. Finally, the SBP annuity is protected against inflation, increasing each December with a Cost of Living Adjustment based on the Consumer Price Index.

Advantage: You can pay for SBP benefits with a pre-tax payroll deduction
For nearly all retirees, Survivor Benefit Plan premiums are automatically deducted from your gross pay prior to the deduction of federal income tax. This decreases your total taxable income.

Disadvantage: Cost
SBP coverage is supplied at no cost while you are in active service. During your retirement, however, a monthly deduction is taken from your pay to pay for your SBP coverage. This can be as much as, but no more than, 6.5 percent of your gross retired pay.

You might consider the relationship between the cost of the program and its benefits. To earn an even return on your investment, your beneficiary typically must receive payment for seven months for every five years you pay SBP premiums..

Disadvantage: Once you enroll, changing your election is difficult
Although it may seem unnecessary to consider providing for your loved ones until later on in life, please be aware that the decisions you make at retirement regarding your SBP can be difficult to change. For example, if, at retirement, you have an eligible spouse or children and decide not to

have them covered under the plan, it will be very difficult to have your current or any future spouse or children covered under the plan in the future.

Cost

The Survivor Benefit Plan cost depends on the level of coverage you choose. SBP coverage is supplied at no cost while you are in active service. During your retirement, however, a monthly deduction is taken from your pay to pay for your SBP coverage. This can be no more than 6.5 percent of your gross retired pay. Review the coverage levels below.

Full Coverage

If you elect full coverage, the cost of SBP coverage will be based on your full gross pay. For example, if you receive $1,000 of retired pay each month, and elect full SBP coverage, your monthly cost to cover your spouse under the plan will be $65 each month.

Reduced Coverage

You can also elect a lower level of SBP coverage. For example, if you receive $1,000 of retired pay each month, you can elect to have your coverage based only on $700 of your pay. In this case, we would calculate 6.5 percent of $700, and the monthly cost to cover a spouse under SBP would be $45.50. There is, however, a minimum level of coverage required and that the amount is unique to each retiree. **(Forrest's note: if you elect a coverage level that is less than full coverage, your spouse will be required to provide a notarized signature—this is indicated below).**

Automatic

If you submit an invalid election at retirement, or none at all, one will be started automatically. The cost of such coverage will be based on gross retired pay and be equal to the cost of a Spouse Only election.

Examples of invalid elections are:

- Non-receipt of a DD 2656 form
- DD 2656 forms signed and/or submitted after retirement

- Declining coverage, or electing any level of coverage lesser than Full Spouse coverage, without a spouse's concurring, notarized signature
- Spouse signing election prior to the member's signature

If we find out later on that you have an eligible spouse and children, the children will be retroactively added to the account and the additional cost for children will be deducted from your pay.

Similarly, if we establish an automatic election and learn later that you have no eligible beneficiaries, we will cancel the election and refund any costs paid.

Eligible Beneficiaries

When you apply for retirement, you will be asked to complete a Data for Payment of Retired Personnel form (DD 2656). On that form, you will need to choose a type of beneficiary. The types you may choose from are described below.

Spouse Only

The most common election for a retiree to make is for only his or her spouse to be covered based on full retired pay. Cost is calculated at a maximum of 6.5 percent of the elected level of coverage.

If you have an eligible spouse and you choose anything less than full coverage, the spouse's notarized signature must be obtained for the election to be considered valid.

Spouse and Children

With this option, all children are covered in equal shares. If you have children at the time of your election, and chose some coverage other than spouse and children, you will not be able to change that election later.

An eligible dependent child under the plan must be:

- Your legal child
- Under the age of 18
- If older than 18, enrolled in an accredited college or university
- Unmarried

Children enrolled in higher education are eligible until they reach age 22 or leave school.

Incapacitated or disabled children are eligible. An incapacitated or disabled child is defined as a child who is incapable of self-support because of a physical or mental disability which existed before the 18th birthday or which was incurred before age 22 while child was pursuing a full-time course of study.

Adding eligible children to an SBP election will add to the cost. The additional cost depends on the age of the retiree, spouse and the youngest child.

Former Spouse

Please keep these factors in mind when considering SBP coverage for a former spouse.

1. Former Spouse Election at the Time of Your Retirement

    a. If you have a former spouse when you first retire and become eligible to participate in the SBP, then you may elect former spouse coverage. (Please note different rules apply for reservists, because of their opportunity to participate in Reserve Component SBP when they receive their 20-year letter.)

    b. If you're married when you become eligible to participate in the SBP and have been court-ordered to cover a former spouse, you can do so without your current spouse's signature.

    c. If you're married at the time you become eligible to participate in the SBP, but you want to voluntarily cover your former spouse, DFAS will be required to notify your current spouse of that election.

    d. You may elect coverage for your former spouse at the time of your retirement even if you divorced more than a year before your retirement and becoming eligible to participate in the SBP.

2. Former Spouse Coverage after retirement

If you've already retired and you want to elect former spouse coverage, or the court has ordered you to do so, you must make a former spouse election within one year of your divorce decree.

3. Your Former Spouse's Right to Request SBP Coverage (aka "Deemed" Election Requests)

If you've been court ordered to elect former spouse SBP, then your former spouse can submit his/her own request to DFAS for former spouse SBP coverage. This is known as a "deemed election request."

Even if you divorced more than a year before retirement, your former spouse can submit a deemed election request, but the request must be submitted within one year of the order requiring former spouse SBP coverage.

If your former spouse submits a proper deemed election request within one year of the court order requiring former spouse SBP coverage, then former spouse SBP coverage will be entered on your account, even if you don't make a former spouse election.

Children Only

If you're married and you choose not to cover your spouse, you must get concurrence from your spouse. If your spouse concurs by signing the form, or if you are unmarried, you can elect to cover your dependent children.

The cost for this option depends on the age of the retiree and the youngest child.

Natural Interest Person (NIP)

If you have no other eligible dependents, you can elect to cover an individual in whom you have a legitimate insurable interest. Examples might be a brother or sister, or a child who is beyond eligibility for child coverage.

Although the annuity benefits of NIP coverage are the same (55 percent of covered pay), the cost (10 percent of your gross pay) is considerably higher than other elections.

Unlike other SBP elections, NIP coverage can be cancelled any time.

A retiree can only elect NIP coverage at retirement.

No Beneficiary

If you do not have any eligible beneficiaries, you are not required to elect coverage at the time of retirement. It is necessary, however, for you to tell us you have no beneficiaries, rather than simply not making an election.

Decline

If you do not consider SBP a worthwhile investment, you may elect not to participate. If you are married and decline to cover your spouse, you must obtain your spouse's notarized signature. In this case, no deductions will be taken from your pay and no benefits will be paid after your death.

Changing or Stopping Your Coverage

The SBP election you make at the time of your retirement is very difficult to change. There are only a few circumstances in which it is possible to change or alter a previously made election. Please review the list below carefully to learn when you can change an SBP election and when you cannot. **(Forrest's note: This is literally what the website says. I'm not sure what list DFAS is referring to, and I was not able to get any response from DFAS when I asked the question).**

To make this change, please complete a Survivor Benefit Plan Election Change Certificate (DD 2656-6) and mail or fax it to DFAS R&A Pay.

Enrolling After Retirement

Some service members choose not to enroll in the SBP plan because they have no eligible beneficiaries at the time of their retirement. Later, through marriage or the birth of a child, they find themselves with eligible beneficiaries and want to change their earlier election.

If this happens to you, you have one year from the date of initial eligibility -- the date of marriage or the birth date of the child -- to declare your wishes to have the beneficiary covered.

To do so, please mail or fax the following items to DFAS Retired and Annuitant Pay within one year of the date of eligibility:

- Survivor Benefit Plan Election Change Certificate (DD 2656-6)
- a copy of any relevant legal document (e.g., marriage certificate or birth certificate)

If you have eligible beneficiaries at the time of your retirement and elect not to have them covered, you will not be able to change that election in the future.

Educate Your Beneficiaries

It's important for your survivors to understand how the Survivor Benefit Plan (SBP) works. Please print this page and share it with your designated beneficiary.

The Nature and Extent of the SBP Benefit

The Survivor Benefit Plan (SBP) provides eligible beneficiaries with a monthly payment known as an annuity. The amount of the benefit is a percentage of your retired pay and it depends upon whether you choose full or reduced coverage. The recipient of your SBP annuity is referred to as the annuitant.

The Benefit's Duration

The SBP entitlement begins upon your death and ends either when your elected beneficiary becomes ineligible to receive the annuity or when your beneficiary dies.

Reasons Payment May Be Temporarily Stopped

Each year we mail annuitants a Certificate of Eligibility (COE). We use the information we request on that form to determine an annuitant's continued eligibility for monthly payments. If we don't receive the COE to by the deadline on the form, we will stop all payments until we receive a properly completed COE (see instructions). If you have not received a COE from us recently and feel you should have, please call us to request one at 800-321-1080.

Reasons Payment Can Be Permanently Stopped

Annuity payments stop when your beneficiary dies or becomes ineligible to receive the annuity. For example, payments stop for children covered under the SBP annuity when they reach age 18. Payments also stop for spouses covered under SBP if they remarry before age 55.

Continuing Children's Benefits after Age 18

Payments typically stop for children covered under SBP when they reach age 18. If a child attends school in a full time status at an accredited college or university, the payments will continue until they reach age 22. Each semester, we mail a Child Annuitant's School Certification form to verify the child is still enrolled. If we don't receive the form by the deadline listed, we will stop all payments until we receive a properly completed form (see instructions). The SBP annuity will terminate at any time if the child remarries. If you have not received a School Certification recently and feel you should have, please call us to request one at 800-321-1080.

Effects of Remarriage on an Annuity

If the annuitant remarries before age 55, annuity payments will stop. However, if the annuitant's marriage later ends, for any reason, even after age 55, the annuity payment will restart from the date the marriage ends.

The annuitant is responsible for notifying DFAS Cleveland of any changes to their marital status.

Benefits from the Department of Veterans' Affairs (VA)

Dependency and Indemnity Compensation (DIC) is an award offered by the VA.

Annuitants cannot receive both SBP and DIC concurrently. When DFAS is informed that an annuitant is eligible to receive DIC from the VA, DFAS will deduct the amount of DIC received from the amount of SBP. For example, if an annuitant receives a monthly annuity of $500 from DFAS and becomes eligible to receive a monthly DIC award of $400 from the VA, DFAS will deduct the $400 DIC from the $500 SBP and pay the remaining $100 to the annuitant.

If the SBP is greater than the DIC award, a partial refund of premiums paid into the program during the service member's retirement will be made. If the DIC payment is greater than the SBP payment, SBP will be stopped completely and all basic spouse premiums paid into the program during the service member's retirement will be refunded.

To receive concurrent SBP and DIC payments, the annuitant must not only be eligible for both, but the DIC entitlement must be a result of a remarriage after the age of 57.

What initiates the SBP benefit and what will my beneficiary have to do?

Your designated beneficiary becomes eligible to receive SBP benefits on the day after your death. The first step a beneficiary must take to initiate receipt of benefits is to report your death. Please visit our Reporting a Death page for step-by-step instructions.

What happens if there is a delay in reporting a retiree's death?

Late notification of a retiree's death may result in burdensome consequences, including delays in finalizing a member's account, payment of arrears of pay and the establishment of an SBP annuity. A retiree's entitlement to retired pay ends on the date he or she dies. Therefore, delayed reporting of a retiree's death may result in an overpayment that will be collected from a financial institution, the member's estate, or from the annuitant if the annuitant is found to be in receipt of the retired pay funds.

Ending SBP after Retirement

You are free to cancel or terminate your SBP election from the 25th month through the 36th month - or the third year - of your retirement. Please note that this window is an exit only, not an entrance, meaning that it applies only to withdrawing from an unwanted election and does not allow retirees to begin an election that they had earlier declined. As with declining at retirement, spousal concurrence is required.

If you believe you are eligible, please complete a Survivor Benefit Plan Termination Request (DD 2656-2) and mail or fax it to DFAS Retired and Annuitant Pay.

What Happens When You Die

It is extremely important for someone to notify DFAS as soon as possible after you die. Late notification of your death could result in burdensome consequences for your survivors, including delays in finalizing your account, paying your Arrears of Pay (AOP) and establishing a Survivor Benefit Plan (SBP) annuity.

Because your entitlement to retired pay ends on the date of your death, delayed reporting also could result in an overpayment that would be collected from your bank, your estate or one of your survivors, if that survivor receives any of your retired pay funds.

Instructions for Your Beneficiary

Please read our instructions for reporting the death of a military retiree. Print them out and give a copy to your SBP beneficiary.

Once your death has been reported, your beneficiary will receive a Verification for Survivor Annuity form (DD 2656-7) at the address we have on record. Your beneficiary must complete the form and return it to us. When we receive the completed form, we will begin the SBP annuity.

Please review our Applying for SBP instructions, print them out and give a copy to your SBP beneficiary.

More information for your SBP beneficiary and other loved ones is available on our Survivors and Beneficiaries pages.

Divorce

A divorce's impact on SBP election depends not only on your wishes, but also on the requirements imposed by the court-ordered divorce decree.

If your divorce decree contains no language mandating you to elect Former Spouse coverage, then you have complete freedom to either have the former spouse removed from the plan or to voluntarily continue the coverage.

If you remove your former spouse from the plan, any premiums deducted beyond the date of divorce will be refunded. If you choose to voluntarily cover your former spouse under the plan, you have until one year after the date of divorce to do so.

If your divorce decree requires you to cover your former spouse, either you or your former spouse must declare your intentions to claim Former Spouse SBP coverage in writing within one year of the date of divorce. To do this, please complete a SBP Election Statement for Former Spouse Coverage (DD 2656-1) and mail or fax it to DFAS Retired and Annuitant Pay.

Death of a Spouse

The death of a spouse covered under the plan results in immediate termination of coverage for that spouse. If the spouse alone was covered, cost will terminate and any premiums paid beyond the date of death will be refunded. If the spouse was covered with children, the election and its costs will change so that only the eligible children are covered.

Remarriage

Changes to your account upon remarriage will depend upon whether you were married at retirement.

If you were married and elected Full Spouse coverage at retirement, you can notify us at any time of your remarriage and a new Full Spouse election will automatically begin effective one year after that marriage date. Spousal concurrence must be obtained to begin coverage at any level lower than the original Spouse election.

If you were married at retirement and elected not to cover your spouse, you cannot ever cover another spouse throughout retirement.

If you were not married at retirement, you must notify us of your intentions to add your spouse to the plan within one year of your marriage. The election will become effective and premium costs will begin to be deducted upon your first anniversary.

To make changes to your spouse election, please complete a Survivor Benefit Plan Election Change Certificate (DD 2656-6) and mail or fax it to DFAS R&A Pay.

Birth of a Child

Upon the birth of a new child, please inform us by supplying us with a copy of the birth certificate.

If you had no children at retirement, we will add the child to the plan and an additional, nominal amount will be added to your monthly premium.

If you did have children at retirement and elected to cover them under the plan, we will add this youngest child and recalculate your cost based on a factor considering your age and the age of this child.

If you had children at retirement and elected not to cover them, any new or existing children will not be covered under the plan throughout your retirement.

Open Season

Only a decision by Congress to initiate a free period of enrollment called an "Open Season" would allow a retiree to begin a new election after retirement. Such periods are rare. The most recent Open Season was in 2005. During this period, everyone who took advantage was required to "buy-in" to the program, meaning they paid an amount equal to the total of all premiums they would have paid if they had enrolled when they first became eligible.

Same-Sex Marriage SBP

On June 26, 2013, the U.S. Supreme Court determined certain parts of Defense of Marriage Act (DOMA) of 1996 were unconstitutional. As a result of this decision, the Federal Government now recognizes same-sex marriages which are legally performed under state law. On September 5, 2013, the Department of Defense (DoD) issued implementing guidance extending Survivor Benefit Plan (SBP) coverage to same-sex spouses of military members and retirees. In short, same-sex marriages that are valid in the state where performed will be recognized as valid for SBP purposes. The implementing guidance does not apply to civil unions or domestic partnerships. It is the responsibility of the retiree to provide documentation of existence of valid marriage under applicable state law. The guidance issued at that time is still applicable to those retirees.

On June 26, 2015 the Supreme Court determined that states are required to issue marriage licenses to two people of the same sex and to recognize a marriage between two people of the same sex when their marriage was lawfully licensed and performed out-of-state. Consequently, a valid marriage certificate issued by any state on or after June 26, 2015 will be recognized as valid for SBP purposes.

The DoD guidance generally provides that effective June 26, 2013, any person who is married to a same-sex partner may participate in the SBP in the same manner as any other married person. This includes the requirement for spousal concurrence for certain elections. The DoD guidance can be read in full here. The below is not a full restatement of the guidance, and is not intended to replace the guidance:

- Any claims to SBP spouse coverage for same-sex spouses of eligible participants of the SBP for periods before June 26, 2013, are not valid as the Defense of Marriage Act was still the law and in effect prior to June 26, 2013. As a result, no SBP premiums for such coverage will be charged prior to that date. Further, no SBP annuity payments for such coverage will be paid for deaths occurring before that date.

- Effective from June 26, 2013, a person who becomes eligible to participate under 10 U.S.C. 1448 (a)(1) and is married to a same-sex partner shall have the SBP program applied as for any other married couple under section 10 U.S.C. 1448, including the requirements for spousal consent for less than full annuity coverage of the spouse. Effective June 26, 2015, there is no need to determine if any particular state permits same sex marriage. Any marriage license issued from a state is presumed valid.

- A person who was married to a same-sex partner upon becoming eligible to participate in the plan prior to June 26, 2013, and who had married that same-sex partner before June 26, 2013, shall have one year from June 26, 2013, to make a spouse election under 10 U.S.C. 1448(a)(3). Such person may not participate at less than maximum coverage described in 10 U.S.C. 1448(a)(3) without the concurrence of the person's spouse unless they already had provided an annuity for a dependent child. If an election is not received on or before June 25, 2014, full spousal coverage shall be entered and the member shall be responsible for payment of premiums effective from June 26, 2013.

- A person who is married to a same-sex partner on June 26, 2013 and has insurable interest coverage under the SBP may terminate the insurable interest coverage and elect spouse coverage. This election must be received on or before June 25, 2014.

- A person who was not married upon becoming eligible to participate in the plan, but who married a same-sex partner before June 26, 2013, shall have one year from June 26, 2013, to make a spouse election under 10 U.S.C. 1448(a)(5). The election must be received on or before June 25, 2014, or the person shall be prohibited by law from making such election.

- Generally, a person who is a participant in the plan and is providing coverage under the SBP for a spouse, who later does not have an eligible spouse beneficiary may, under 10 U.S.C. 1448(a)(6), elect not to provide coverage for a new spouse in the event of a remarriage.

- For a person who enters into a same-sex marriage after June 26, 2013, the election to discontinue participation under 10 U.S.C. 1448(a)(6) must be made within one year of the remarriage. If a member does not discontinue participation, then pursuant to 10 U.S.C. 1448(a)(6), spouse coverage will resume effective on the first anniversary of the marriage.

- If the remarriage took place prior to June 26, 2013, the participant has one year from June 26, 2013 to elect out of SBP. If a member does not make such an election within one year of June 26, 2013, then pursuant to section 10 U.S.C. 1448(a)(6), spouse coverage will resume effective no earlier than June 25, 2014.

- Additionally, any such person falling within the parameters of section 10 U.S.C. 1448(g), shall have one year from June 26, 2013, or the date of any marriage subsequent to that date, to elect to increase the level of coverage under 10 U.S.C. 1448(g).

Note: Any person eligible to participate (either already retired and receiving retired pay or in receipt of a 20-year letter and awaiting pay), who was not married at the time they become eligible to participate and who marries *after* June 26, 2015, has one year from the date of the marriage to enter a spousal election for SBP purposes.

Survivor Benefit Plan Enrollment

As you prepare for retirement, it is very important to seek counseling from your Branch of Service on your options.

First, you should review <u>DD Form 2656</u>: Data for Payment of Retired Personnel.

The DD 2656 offers brief instructions regarding election options and requirements, but you also need to consider other implications. Please make the time to carefully review information about <u>SBP Elections and Eligible Beneficiaries</u>.

When you have made your decisions and are signing Form DD2656, please keep in mind:

- The form must be signed prior to your retirement date
- Your witness must sign the document on the same date as you
- If a spouse's signature is required, it must be on or after the date of your signature, but also before your retirement date
- The notary witnessing the spouse's signature must sign the document on the same date as the spouse

Paying for SBP

There are four methods of paying for your SBP coverage if you elect it:

- Deductions from your retired pay
- Deductions from your VA pay
- Direct remittance
- Paid Up Status

Deductions from your Retired Pay (Normal Payment Method)

The normal method of paying for SBP coverage is by an automatic deduction from your retirement pay. The vast majority of retired members with SBP coverage pay through this means. It is implemented automatically if you elect SBP coverage at the time you retire.

Deductions from your VA Pay

If you have been ruled severely disabled by the Department of Veterans Affairs (VA) and your VA compensation exceeds your retired pay, you don't receive retired pay from DFAS. As a result, we cannot automatically deduct SBP premiums from your monthly pay. (See Disability Entitlements for information about the Branch of Service/VA offset),

In this case, the best way to pay for your SBP coverage is to have your payments deducted from your VA compensation and forwarded to DFAS Retired and Annuitant Pay by the VA. Thousands of retirees take advantage of this process.If you are interested in taking part, please have the VA help you complete an Authorization for SBP Cost Deduction (DD 2891) and mail or fax it to the Direct Remittance address listed below.

Direct Remittance

Direct remittance is only for those retired members who do not receive retired pay from DFAS or who do not receive enough retired pay to pay for SBP premiums. Direct remittance members who choose not to have their

SBP payments deducted from their VA pay must remit SBP premium payments directly to:

Defense Finance and Accounting Service, DFAS-CL
SBP and RSFPP Remittance
P.O. Box 979013
St. Louis, MO 63197-9000

Payments sent to any other location, including Retired and Annuitant Pay offices at DFAS Cleveland, will not be received. Any delinquent amounts carried over into a new billing month will accrue an interest fee calculated at 6 percent Annual Percentage Yield.

Paid Up Status

Beginning Oct. 1, 2008, any retiree who has paid 360 months of SBP premiums and has reached the age of 70 is no longer be required to make monthly payments for their SBP coverage. If you meet these requirements, your SBP election and account will remain active, and benefits to annuitants will be uninterrupted, but there will be no further cost to you. To help you track your status, Retiree Account Statements (RAS) include a "premium counter" indicating the number of months of paid premiums credited to your account.

Updating Your SBP Beneficiary Designations

It is important to notify us as soon as possible when a beneficiary change occurs. Events like divorce or remarriage change the beneficiary status of your account. If you have not notified us of changes like this, you may have an invalid beneficiary designation. In the event of your death, we would be required to spend time identifying and then locating your rightful beneficiary. This would make it difficult or even impossible to process the benefit claim quickly, and might create a financial hardship for your loved ones.

Failing to Update Your SBP Beneficiary Could Have Financial Consequences

Making sure that we are aware of any changes in your beneficiaries will benefit you as well. If you do not inform us of a divorce, you could forfeit a refund of overpaid premiums. DFAS is barred by law from refunding payments retroactively beyond a six-year period. If a retiree divorces a spouse and does not notify us until 10 years after the fact, we will only be able to refund six years of those payments.

How to Update Your SBP Beneficiary Designations

To change or update your SBP beneficiary designation, please complete a Survivor Benefit Plan Election Change Certificate (DD 2656-6).

Legal documents such as marriage certificates, divorce decrees and birth certificates are essential to processing changes of beneficiary or claims under SBP. Forms and legal documents can be faxed or mailed to:

Defense Finance and Accounting Service
U.S. Military Retirement Pay
P.O. Box 7130
London, KY 40742-7130

Fax: 800-469-6559

Please only send copies of documents. Do not send the originals.

Appendix Two: OSD Office of the Actuary Website Links

Office of the Actuary: http://actuary.defense.gov

Subsidy:
http://actuary.defense.gov/LinkClick.aspx?fileticket=nC1vbNNdto4%3d&tabid=1731&portalid=15

Insurance:
http://actuary.defense.gov/LinkClick.aspx?fileticket=q4WHwEDh0bY%3d&tabid=1732&portalid=15

Premium:

http://actuary.defense.gov/LinkClick.aspx?fileticket=JOz34BnfcK8%3d&tabid=1733&portalid=15

Probability:

http://actuary.defense.gov/LinkClick.aspx?fileticket=0UgCGCIGMFc%3d&tabid=1778&portalid=15

Appendix Three: OSD and Service-Specific SBP Instructions

- DOD Instruction 1332.42: Survivor Annuity Program Administration:
  http://www.dtic.mil/whs/directives/corres/pdf/133242p.pdf

- Army: AR 600-8-7-Retirement Services Program:
  http://www.apd.army.mil/pdffiles/r600_8_7.pdf

- Navy: OPNAV Instruction 1750.5A-Survivor Benefit Plan Program:
  https://doni.daps.dla.mil/Directives/01000%20Military%20Person
  nel%20Support/01-
  700%20Morale,%20Community%20and%20Religious%20Service
  s/1750.5A.pdf

- Air Force: AFI 36-3006-Survivor Benefit Plan (SBP) and Supplemental Survivor Benefit Plan (SSBP):
  http://webapp1.dlib.indiana.edu/virtual_disk_library/index.cgi/821
  003/FID177/pubs/af/36/afi36-3006/afi36-3006.pdf

- Marines: Marine Corps Order 1741.11D-Survivor Annuity Program – Survivor Benefit Plans (SBP):
  http://www.marines.mil/Portals/59/MCO%201741_11D.pdf

[i] Defense Financial & Accounting Service, Cleveland Guide to Survivor Benefits Reserve Component Survivor Benefit Plan (RCSBP), Retired Serviceman's Family Protection Plan (RSFPP), and Survivor Benefit Plan (SBP), August 2013, http://www.dfas.mil/dam/jcr:fbbe66f5-e3c2-4e17-90d2-7681e1de3ddc/Draft_SBP_Guide_Book_Aug_2014_20150323.pdf

[ii] Department of Labor, "Labor Force Participation Rates by Sex and Race or Hispanic Ethnicity, 1972-2012," http://www.dol.gov/wb/stats/facts_over_time.htm#labor

[iii] Pew Research Center, "Breadwinner Moms," May 29, 2013, http://www.pewsocialtrends.org/2013/05/29/breadwinner-moms/

[iv] World Bank, Life Expectancy at Birth, Total (years), http://data.worldbank.org/indicator/SP.DYN.LE00.IN

[v] World Bank, Health Expenditure, Total (% of GDP), http://data.worldbank.org/indicator/SH.XPD.TOTL.ZS

[vi] "Health Expenditure Trends in OECD Countries, 1970-1997," Manfred Huber, Ph.D., Health Care Financing Review/Winter 1999/Volume 21, Number 2; Centers for Medicare and Medicaid Services https://www.cms.gov/Research-Statistics-Data-and-Systems/Research/HealthCareFinancingReview/downloads/99winterpg99.pdf

[vii] "The Percentage of College Graduates Has Soared Since 1965," Familyfacts.org website chart, http://www.familyfacts.org/charts/560/the-percentage-of-college-graduates-has-soared-since-1965

[viii] "Tuition and Fees and Room and Board over Time, 1975-1976 to 2015-2016, Selected Years," Collegeboard.org website, http://trends.collegeboard.org/college-pricing/figures-tables/tuition-and-fees-and-room-and-board-over-time-1975-76-2015-16-selected-years#Key%20Points

[ix] Debt.org website, https://www.debt.org/students/

[x] "144 Years of Marriage and Divorce in the United States, in One Chart," Ana Swanson, Washington Post, June 23, 2015; https://www.washingtonpost.com/news/wonk/wp/2015/06/23/144-years-of-marriage-and-divorce-in-the-united-states-in-one-chart/